ONCE IN
28 YEARS

ONCE IN 28 YEARS

THE BLESSING OF THE SUN — BIRKAS HACHAMAH

A TARGUM PRESS BOOK

First published 2009
Copyright © 2009 by Moshe Goldberger
P.O. Box 82
Staten Island, NY 10309
718-948-2548
rabbig@sakar.com
ISBN 978-1-56871-481-3

Published and distributed by:
TARGUM PRESS, INC.
22700 W. Eleven Mile Rd.
Southfield, MI 48034
E-mail: targum@targum.com
Fax: 888-298-9992
www.targum.com

Distributed by:
FELDHEIM PUBLISHERS
208 Airport Executive Park
Nanuet, NY 10954

Printing plates by Frank, Jerusalem
Printed in Israel by Chish

For my dear father,
Yaakov ben Feigel

For my dear mother,
Dvoshke bas Fraydl

and for myself,
Yitzchok ben Dvoshke

In loving memory of my dear sister
Feigel bas Yaakov
who was *nifteres* on *erev Pesach*, April 5, 1993.

May none of us know any further sorrow.

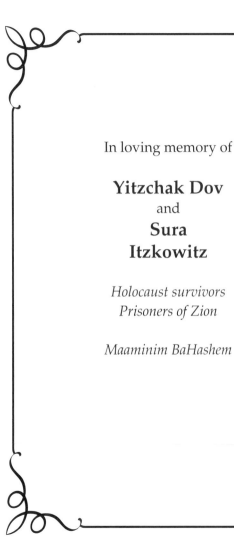

In loving memory of

Yitzchak Dov
and
**Sura
Itzkowitz**

*Holocaust survivors
Prisoners of Zion*

Maaminim BaHashem

on the wonderful occasion of his
bar mitzvah.

Just as the sun continuously follows the
Almighty's command while only receiving
special acknowledgment every twenty-
eight years, so too may you continue to
give us all *nachas* as your Torah learning is
only outshone by your *middos*.

Mazal tov!!!
We love you,

Uncle Ari, Auntie Malkie,
Yehuda, Sari, and Ayala

Dedicated by

The U.S. / Israel Venture Summit

An annual investment conference uniting Israel's most exciting stage and emerging companies with private and institutional investors.

Joseph Benjamin
www.youngstartup.com
718-447-0817

My loving father,

יעקב בן ציון בן זלמן זצ״ל

Who encouraged me and taught me all my life.

My wonderful husband,

הרב יעקב בן שמואל זצ״ל

Who loved learning and teaching *Yiddishkeit*, and
left a legacy of caring and מדות טובות to his children,
and grandchildren.

Dedicated in their honor by their loving wife,
daughter, and granddaughter

אייגא שרה Pianko, **מרים רחל** Burstein,
חיה ביילא Gelman, and their families

WITH THANKS TO:

Yitzchok E. Gold
David Goldberger
Binyamin Siegel
Charles S. Mamiye
Bob Burg
Mordechai Kairey
Dr. J. Cohen
Isak Boruchin
Rabbi Zecharia Weitz
Mrs. Chaya Baila Gavant
Mrs. Bassi Gruen
and others

Part III: The Message

Every day we recite various blessings to thank Hashem for returning our souls, giving us the Torah, opening our eyes, granting us understanding, providing us with clothing, providing all of our needs, and on and on. In addition, we say a general blessing, "*Yotzer Ohr*," to thank Hashem for the creation of the sun and the entire world.

But a special blessing for the sun, *Birkas HaChamah*, is said only once every twenty-eight years. The next time this blessing will be said, *im yirtzeh Hashem*, is Wednesday, April 8, 2009 (14 Nissan, 5769); the next time after that, twenty-eight years later, will be Wednesday, April 8, 2037 (23 Nissan, 5797). (This blessing is always recited on a Wednesday, the fourth day of the week, and is currently always on April 8 because it is related to the solar year.)

On occasion, you may hear someone discussing his or her favorite Jewish holiday or observance. He or she may say, "Rosh HaShanah," "Sukkos," or "Pesach." But who describes their favorite mitzvah as *"Birkas HaChamah"*?

The truth is, though, that every holiday or observance in Jewish life is an opportunity for introspection and growth in many ways. Like most opportunities, it has to be recognized, studied, and embraced; otherwise it may slip away.

What is the meaning of the *berachah* of *Birkas HaChamah*?

Why do we make this *berachah*?

Why do we only recite it once every twenty-eight years?

Does the number twenty-eight have some intrinsic meaning?

What if it is cloudy or raining on the morning of April 8, 2009?

What have we been doing with our lives for the past twenty-eight years?

What should another hour, day, month, year, twenty-eight years mean to us?

What should we hope and expect to accomplish, *b'ezras Hashem*, in the next twenty-eight years?

How can this blessing for the sun serve as a model

for us to focus on similar opportunities as well?

Who is wise? He who foresees the future.

(*Tamid* 32a)

If you look at chapter 28 of this book, you will see that it provides you with food for thought about your plans. Which plans are these? That is for you to determine.

First calculate how many weeks are left until April 8, 2009. (If that date has already passed, the next opportunity for this mitzvah will be on April 8, 2037.) Then make a schedule of how many pages you will need to read each week before *Birkas HaChamah* arrives so that you can digest the material before that day. In this way, you will gain the most from this book — and from this unique mitzvah.

PART I
THE MITZVAH

What is the source for the mitzvah of *Birkas Ha-chamah*?

The Gemara states:

> *One who sees the sun at the beginning of its cycle... should say, "Blessed [are You, Hashem]...Who makes [the work of] Creation."*
>
> (*Berachos* 59b)

When is the beginning of the sun's cycle? The Gemara continues,

> *Every twenty-eight years the cycle begins again, when the Nissan equinox falls [on the evening of Tuesday going into Wednesday]...*
>
> (Ibid.)

We learn from this that we say the *berachah* upon seeing the sun on a Wednesday morning after the vernal equinox (the *"tekufah"*) every twenty-eight years, in commemoration of the sun's creation. (See *Shulchan Aruch*, *Orach Chaim* 229:2.)

The twenty-eight-year cycle is based upon the concept that a solar year is 365¼ days long. The sun returns to its basic original position annually, but we say the blessing only when it returns to its original position on the same day of the week and at the same time of day as it was in at the time of Creation, which occurs only once in twenty-eight years (since 28 quarters equals 7, the number of the days of the week). (See *The Jewish Calendar*, by Rabbi David Feinstein, [New York: Mesorah Publications, 2004], pp. 162–163.)

Every twenty-eight years, the sun and the planets reach the position they were in when Hashem first placed them in their orbits, at the time of Creation.

Why does this always occur on Wednesday? In *Bereishis* (1:14–19), we learn that Hashem created the sun on day four.

✦ ✦ ✦

This leads us to an interesting question. The Torah tells us that on day one Hashem created light and darkness (see *Bereishis* 1:4). When did that light

that the first light was created before the sun was positioned to teach us that light and all other natural phenomena are emanations of the Creator's glory.

ONE MOMENT SPOTLIGHT: The primary source of the *Birkas HaChamah* blessing comes from five lines in the Gemara (*Berachos* 59b), as expounded by Rashi and other commentators.

If you do not already have a *chavrusa*, study partner, set one up now so that you can study the original Gemara and the comments of Rashi. You can master it if you plan for it and focus on it. In addition, once you have studied the material in the original sources, you may have new insights that will enhance your enjoyment of the service, as well as your enjoyment of life, with Hashem's help.

Chapter 2
THE HALACHOS OF BIRKAS HACHAMAH

THE BASIC HALACHAH

One who sees the sun at the beginning of its cycle, i.e., once every twenty-eight years when our Sages tells us it is back at the position it was in at the time of Creation, when the sun comes up, recites the blessing *"Oseh Ma'aseh Vereishis"*:

> *Baruch Atah Hashem Elokeinu Melech HaOlam, oseh ma'aseh vereishis* — Blessed are You, Hashem, our G-d, King of the Universe, who makes the work of Creation.

One caveat: It is not necessary — moreover, it is dangerous — to stare into the sun before or after saying the *berachah*. All that is necessary is to glance at the sun briefly.

At what time(s) one can say the *berachah* on April 8, 2009, and (2) what happens if one cannot see the sun that day — i.e., it's cloudy or raining.

The Chasam Sofer refers to the *Birkas HaChamah* preparations in 1813 (5573) when many people asked whether they could say the *berachah* even without seeing the sun, i.e., if the sun was obscured.

He answers that this is not permitted. The only leniency he consents to is saying the blessing when the sun is covered by clouds but an impression of it can still be seen, as his rebbe, Rav Nosson Adler, ruled in 1785/5545.

Further, if one does not even see the impression of the sun, the Chasam Sofer rules that he may not recite any *berachah*, even without Hashem's Name.

If it is later than three hours after sunrise and one sees the impression of the sun, the Chasam Sofer rules that one can say the *berachah*, but without Hashem's Name. (On this point the *Mishnah Berurah* disagrees, stating that one can rely on many other opinions to even say the *berachah* with Hashem's Name at that time.)

Based on this discussion, the halachah is as follows:

The *berachah* should ideally be recited with a multitude of people (*Mishnah Berurah* 229:2), for the verse states, "With a multitude of people there is more glory to the King" (*Mishlei* 14:28).

On a clear day, the custom is to recite the *berachah* after *shacharis*, morning prayers. The best time to say the *berachah*, however, is at sunrise, which differs from place to place, or the earlier the better after that.

On a cloudy day, if a person sees the sun earlier than he would with a minyan, he should not delay and recite the *berachah* immediately, even by himself.

If a person is unable to say the *berachah* at sunrise, he may say it until *chatzos*, noon. Some say one may only say it up to three *sha'os zemaniyos*, special hours that are based upon the length of the day, after sunrise. After *chatzos*, one may only say the *berachah* without Hashem's Name.

MORE POINTS

It is ideal to say the *berachah* while standing, but this is not required.

Some keep their tallis and tefillin on when reciting

say the blessing. The Kaf HaChaim rules that it is best for them to listen to others saying the *berachah* and be included with them. Many *poskim* rule that women may recite the blessing if they wish to, but there should not be any mingling between men and women.

Children should be trained to say the *berachah* from the age of *chinuch* (six or seven years and up).

The Kaf HaChaim rules that a blind person should not say the *berachah*, but he can be included in the *berachah* of another person, provided that the person saying the *berachah* has the blind person in mind and the listener answers "*amen*" (*Kaf HaChaim* 229:8).

"SHEHECHIYANU"

We do not say the "*Shehechiyanu*" blessing at *Birkas HaChamah*.

This blessing states: "Blessed are You, Hashem…

Who has kept us alive, sustained us, and brought us to this season."

The Sages established various occasions when a person says the *"Shehechiyanu"* blessing — for example, upon buying a significant garment (such as a new suit or a tallis), building or buying a new house, eating a new fruit, or listening to the shofar. However, the blessing of *Birkas HaChamah* is not one of these occasions, even though this opportunity arises only every twenty-eight years.

Some of the reasons for this exclusion are that this *berachah* is in the nature of praise of Hashem, as opposed to giving thanks for some type of physical pleasure. Additionally, the sun looks the same on this special day; we don't see anything unusual about it that would warrant a *"Shehechiyanu."* This *berachah* on Creation is also not unique, since we also say it after seeing lightning and other natural phenomena.

Nevertheless, there is a way to incorporate a *"Shehechiyanu" berachah* if some other valid reason exists for saying it — for example, if one has a new suit or a new fruit.

Any doubts or questions on the halachos should be presented to one's *rav* for clarification.

ONE MOMENT SPOTLIGHT: Why does the halachah

(Avos 5:17)

There are countless halachic discussions and arguments recorded in the Talmud. Why is this so? The oral law, which later became recorded as the Mishnah and the Talmud, was transmitted verbally to Moshe Rabbeinu at Sinai, and over time many issues were clarified and discussed by the sages, often leading to the development of various opinions on small details.

Why did Hashem allow the Torah to develop in such a way? Why didn't He give us everything in one straight shot, written down from the beginning, so that there would be no questions?

One answer is that "these and those are [all] words of the living G-d" (*Eruvin* 13b). Studying Hashem's Torah, both the written and oral laws, for the sake of Heaven is our greatest duty, because this is what enables us to come as close to Hashem as possible. In fact, a person who is an expert in all aspects of the Torah and is a G-d-fearing person with excellent *middos* (character traits) is considered a live *sefer Torah*, who can answer questions and give advice on all subjects of life.

Before reciting the *Birkas HaChamah* blessing, we recite *Tehillim* 148, which begins, "*Hallelukah*, Praise Hashem from the heavens..." Afterwards, the blessing "*Oseh Ma'aseh Vereishis*" is recited, and then the song "*Keil Adon*," followed by *Tehillim* 19, which begins, "The heavens declare the glory of Hashem..." We conclude with "*Aleinu*," followed by Kaddish (if there are ten males present).

✦ ✦ ✦

Why do we refer to *Birkas HaChamah* as a mitzvah? What category of mitzvos is it included in?

Rabbi Simlai said: Six hundred and thirteen mitzvos were conveyed to Moshe, three hundred and sixty-five prohibitions corresponding to the number of days

in the solar year, and two hundred and forty-eight
positive commands corresponding to the number of
limbs in a person's body...

(*Makkos* 23b)

The 613 mitzvos referred to here are listed by the Rambam (in his *Sefer HaMitzvos*) and by the *Sefer HaChinuch*. *Birkas HaChamah* is not on either of these lists, but rather is a *berachah* included in the Rambam's *Hilchos Berachos* (10:18), in the category of praise and thanks to Hashem.

The first of the Ten Commandments includes within it the mitzvah to believe in the existence of the omnipotent Creator and Controller, Hashem. This mitzvah is unique in that it is the first of the six constant mitzvos, those mitzvos that are not restricted to a specific time or place and that apply to every Jew, every minute of every day.

The foundation of all foundations and the pillar of all
wisdom is to know that there is a Creator Who cre-
ated the universe with profound wisdom...

(Rambam, *Hilchos Yesodei HaTorah* 1:1)

(See also *77 Mitzvos for Today*, Targum Press, 2005, pp. 13–14.)

Thus, we can say that *Birkas HaChamah*, like all

the other *berachos* we say, is a reinforcement of the

prepare for the next opportunity to recite this important *berachah*, so that we may all truly gain from this unique opportunity to proclaim, "Blessed are You, Hashem...Who makes the work of Creation," with enthusiasm and thankfulness.

During the repetition of the Shabbos morning *Amidah*, the silent prayer, the congregation stops to recite *Kedushah*, which describes how the angels praise Hashem. One of these verses proclaims: "Then with a great, tumultuous sound, mighty and powerful, they raise their voices... and declare, 'Blessed...' "

Rav Avigdor Miller asks why the verse says, "with a great, tumultous sound." After all, it could simply say, "*kol*, a sound," or "*kol ra'ash*, a tumultuous sound"; but no, it is described as "*kol ra'ash gadol*, a great, tumultuous sound"! He explains that this teaches us that when it comes to praising Hashem, we must initiate a very great tumult, to demonstrate that Hashem is the only entity to be excited about (*The Path of Life*, compiled by Rabbi Yehoshua Danese [Lakewood, NJ: Israel Bookshop, 2002], p. 221).

✦ ✦ ✦

The following chapters will be devoted to examining each of the parts of the *Birkas HaChamah* service so that we will be able to take full advantage of this opportunity, available to us only once in twenty-eight years. In addition, many of these prayers are part of our daily prayers, and this timely review may help us enhance and elevate these prayers as well.

Chapter 148 of *Tehillim*, which we recite each morning, is composed of fourteen verses that focus on all of nature joining in with joyous songs of praise to Hashem. The first six verses focus on the heavens and the last eight focus on the earth. Let us touch on a brief message from each verse:

PART 1: THE HEAVENS

- *Hallelukah, Praise Hashem*… Rav Avigdor Miller explains that the word *hallelukah* means to get enthusiastic and excited over Hashem's greatness, wisdom, and kindness.

- *Praise Hashem from the heavens*… When we study the world and utilize it to praise Hashem, we are bringing it to its ultimate purpose, for everything was created for Hashem's glory (see *Avos* 6:11).

- *Praise Him, all His angels...* There are myriads of angels that all do Hashem's bidding, yet we can inspire them to praise their Creator! The Midrash (*Tanna D'Vei Eliyahu* 3) explains that since we were created with the free will to choose to praise Hashem, our choices cause the entire world to praise Hashem.

- *Praise Him, sun and moon; praise Him, all luminous stars.* This verse is the source for saying this chapter of *Tehillim* as a prelude to the blessing for the sun, which is one of the great servants of Hashem. Have you ever heard of a light bulb that can burn for twenty-eight years without fading?

- *Praise Him, the heavens above the heavens.* The vastness of space teaches us the unlimited greatness of Hashem.

- *They praise the Name of Hashem, for He commanded and they were created.* Hashem gave instructions, and all of the heavenly bodies were created. "Raise up your eyes on high and see Who created these" (*Yeshayah* 40:26).

- *He established it for all time...* Hashem designed a system that is still functioning well after 5,769 years.

PART 2: THE EARTH

perform His word." These are examples of Hashem's magnificent works, each one phenomenal in itself.

The first example, fire or lightning, is related to the sun — each bolt of lightning is like a miniature sliver of sunlight that provides enormous benefits to the earth.

- *The mountains and all hills, fruit trees and all cedars.* Rav Avigdor Miller (*Praise My Soul*, p. 195) lists some of the benefits we gain from mountains and hills: The melting snow from the mountains gradually supplies streams with water; they protect the valleys from wind; they provide fortification for towns and cities; and they help us feel humble before Hashem, when we contemplate the tall mountains that He created, which are huge in comparison to us.

- *Animals and cattle, creeping creatures and birds.*

Hashem created millions of creatures which sing His praises through their very essence and through all of their miraculous components.

- *Kings and nations, leaders and judges…* There is a special blessing recited upon seeing a gentile king, who rules lawfully and has the power of life and death: "Blessed are You, Hashem… Who gives of His glory to flesh and blood" (*Berachos* 58a). This *berachah* serves as a reminder that everything is arranged by the King of the Universe, even the appointment of non-Jewish leaders.

- *Boys and girls, older people and younger people.* Each person has great potential to connect with Hashem at whatever stage he is at, to serve Him and sing His praises.

(The next two verses are also recited when we return the Torah to the Ark.)

- *They shall praise Hashem's Name, for His Name is most exalted; His glory fills the world.* Here, we acknowledge that Hashem is the Eternal Master of All and that every one of His creations needs to thank Him for all of His constant gifts to us.

- *He has given His nation great power, He praises all of*

His pious ones, the Jewish people, whom He consid-

Who guides our every action and we are always responsible to Him.

✦ ✦ ✦

ONE MOMENT SPOTLIGHT: In our daily lives, we tend to lose track of what is important in life. Often, a sales supervisor or business owner may say to a salesperson, "You are not going out to lunch to eat lunch!" When a salesperson takes out a customer, the primary purpose of the meeting is to do business. He must not lose focus and concentrate on the food, rather than on the customer.

The same thing applies to us — we must not lose our focus on the important things in life! We are not here to merely see the flowers. We are here to recognize Who created them, and to praise Him accordingly.

Chapter 5

THE BLESSING OF "OSEH MA'ASEH VEREISHIS"

BEREISHIS — THE BEGINNING

> *Blessed are You, Hashem, our G-d, King of the Universe, Who makes the work of Creation [or, "who creates the work of the beginning"].*

There are many lessons we can learn from this blessing. Let us first focus on the word *bereishis*, the first word of the Chumash and the last word of this blessing, translated as either "Creation" or "the beginning."

The Vilna Gaon (*Safra D'Tzniusa*, quoted in *Machasheves Mussar*, p. 147) writes that all of the Torah and all of history can be seen in the first verse of the Torah and in the first word of that verse, i.e., *bereishis* — the beginning.

Rabbi Elazar Menachem Shach, zt"l (Machasheves

bulbs or batteries to replace or recharge the sun?

Similarly, Hashem created everything in the universe in such a way that nothing ever runs out. There is a water cycle that continually replenishes itself, fruits and grains have seeds which serve as a source for new food, animals and humans reproduce their own kind on a regular basis, and on and on. All this was intended by Hashem at *bereishis*, the beginning. Hashem created the world with built-in systems that enable it to function at top form for as long as He desires it to do so.

✦   ✦   ✦

The blessing of *"Oseh Ma'aseh Vereishis"* is recited not only on the sun, but also whenever we see a shooting star, a comet, lightning, or an earthquake.

What is the similarity between these events and *Birkas HaChamah*? All of these exceptional events offer us a glimpse of Hashem's process of creation. They should all cause us to stop and contemplate the power, wisdom, and kindness of Hashem.

Often, we recite *berachos* from habit, forgetting the great lessons they contain. For example, when we see lightning, we may rush through the *berachah* without even once considering the marvelous reminder of Hashem's greatness we have experienced. When we say a *berachah* to thank and praise Hashem for His creations, we are recognizing His Presence, His love for us, His ongoing help to us, His desire to be close to us, His awesome power, and the fact that He made the world for us and He is always there for us.

Every thing and every person we encounter serve as a reminder for us to think about Hashem.

✦ ✦ ✦

There is a mitzvah to say one hundred blessings each day. (See our book, *One Hundred Berachos* [Brooklyn, NY: Judaica Press, 2001].) Each of these blessings serves to help us think about Hashem.

Don't let blessings fade from your mind without focusing on them. Every *berachah* begins with speaking about Hashem's Name and reminding ourselves that He is the King: "Blessed are You, Hashem, our G-d, King of the Universe..."

We should say every blessing slowly, and think:

on caring for us because He chose us as His beloved children forever.

• *Melech HaOlam*: He is the King of the Universe, always, in complete control.

Whether we are in a hurry or not, we sometimes float through *berachos* with our thoughts focused on the next event in our day — whether it is work, shopping, a conference, or anything else. It is crucial to stop and think what the *berachah* is really saying: This world was created by a Supreme Being Who supplies us with all of our needs.

❖ ❖ ❖

ONE MOMENT SPOTLIGHT: Our Sages explain that the true purpose of life is to bless Hashem (see *Yeshayah* 43:21). A person can sit down to eat lunch, thinking, *Great meal — I don't mind spending a few minutes on the blessings, too*! A truer perspective, however, would be to recognize that the food has been provided for us in order for us to recite the *berachos* that help us appreciate Hashem's great kindnesses.

Imagine saying, "Those blessings were delicious!"

This poetic prayer of praise is taken from the Shabbos morning service, in the blessings for the sun that precede *Kerias Shema*. It is made up of twenty-two phrases, based on the *alef-beis*, which speak of Hashem's greatness and kindness.

These praises are divided into six parts:

PART 1

- *Almighty G-d, Master over all works...* He is the Source of all energy, the sole Manufacturer of every component of every creation. Thus, He is the complete Master.

- *The Blessed One, Who is blessed by every soul.* Why do we use the term *souls*, as opposed to "people" or "creations"? The soul is the true essence of who we are!

- *His greatness and goodness fill the world.* Rav Avigdor Miller used to use this phrase as a guideline to appreciating everything that we see in the world. For example, why are apples red? It is a sign of Hashem's greatness and goodness so that we should know that the apple is ripe and ready to eat — and it tastes better with a beautiful color. A red apple is like a stop sign among the green leaves, proclaiming, "Stop and recognize the Creator."

- *Wisdom and insight surround Him.* His wisdom is evident from everything He created.

PART 2

- *He is exalted above all holy angels....* In other words, He is exalted above all.

- *He is splendid in glory over the [Holy] chariot...* He is splendid above all.

- *Merit and fairness are before His throne.* Although He is most exalted, His focus is always on fairness and the merits of all.

- *Kindness and mercy are in front of His glory.* Hashem's kindness, compassion, and mercy are His true glory, as it says, "The world was built for kindliness" (*Tehillim* 89:3).

PART 3

- *He invested in them strength and power* — Because He is so strong and powerful, He is able to invest these characteristics in His creations.

- *So that they may rule over the world* — Hashem has invested the luminaries with the power of bringing life or causing death, in many ways. The ultimate authority, though, is always Hashem.

PART 4

- *Filled with radiance and radiating brightness.* Again we see the awesome power of the heavenly bodies.

- *Their beauty radiates all over*...benefitting us in countless ways.

- *They are glad as they go out and rejoice as they come in.* The luminaries rejoice in the opportunity to fulfill Hashem's will.

- *They serve their Creator with trepidation.* This is the principle of serving Hashem with joy and trembling, which translates into love and awe (see *Tehillim* 2:11).

PART 5

- *Splendor and glory they offer to His Name* — by their very existence.

- *They ascribe gladness and song to the mention of His authority.* Because all that the Merciful One does is for good, knowing that He is in charge brings us joy.

- *He called to the sun to provide light.* Hashem is the One Who causes the sun to provide us with light each and every day. The sun is not on "cruise control."

- *He saw and fixed the form of the moon.* At first, the moon and the sun were the same size. However, the moon was diminished in size when it complained to Hashem about its role. This serves as a lesson for all time that if a person doesn't appreciate and rejoice with the gifts Hashem has provided for him, he may cause himself to "diminish" also.

PART 6

✦ ✦ ✦

ONE MOMENT SPOTLIGHT: *Keil Adon* is actually recited on three different occasions: (1) on Shabbos morning before *Kerias Shema*, (2) following *Kiddush Levanah* (the sanctification of the new moon), and (3) at *Birkas HaChamah*. Some congregations have the custom to dance while saying *Keil Adon* after *Kiddush Levanah*, as pointed out by the *Shulchan Aruch* (426:2) in the laws of *Kiddush Levanah*.

The *Shulchan Aruch* writes (ibid.) that the Jewish people are compared to the moon and Hashem is compared to the sun. Thus, the renewal of the moon is symbolic of the restoration of the Jewish nation to its former glory, as the moon will eventually be restored to its former greatness, equal to that of the sun. The dancing at

Kiddush Levanah is therefore similar to the dancing of a wedding ceremony.

We sincerely hope that this upcoming *Birkas HaChamah* puts a dance in your steps, an extra bit of happiness as you celebrate being alive and witnessing the wonderful natural phenomena that Hashem has created in the universe for your benefit.

> *Every person must view the world as if Hashem created it especially for him.*
>
> (*Sanhedrin* 37a)

Now that's something to dance about!

While the other chapter of *Tehillim* that we recite in the *Birkas HaChamah* service, *Tehillim* 148, is recited every morning, *Keil Adon* and *Tehillim* 19 are recited during the Shabbos morning service. Shabbos itself serves as the great reminder of Creation, of the fact that Hashem created the world out of nothing. On Shabbos, our morning service is longer in order to reflect upon the day of rest and to contemplate the greatness of Hashem, Who created all.

The fifteen verses of *Tehillim* 19 relate how we learn from Hashem's world and from His Torah to appreciate Him, be aware of Him, love Him, fear Him, and praise Him:

- *For the Conductor, a song by David.* By singing Hashem's praises, we train ourselves to think about Him and to serve Him.

    The word *Conductor* has special significance in

relation to the *Birkas HaChamah* service. When we think of the word *conductor*, it usually brings to mind the idea of an orchestra, consisting of various instruments playing beautiful music together. Similarly, the sun, the planets, the stars, and the solar system work in harmony to remind us of the Ultimate Conductor, who places each of these phenomena in its place for our benefit.

On a broader scale, the orchestra of Hashem is not limited to the heavens above. We are all part of His orchestra, and we must do our best to play the right notes by studying His Torah, performing His mitzvos, and fulfilling our potential.

- *The heavens relate His glory...* When we walk outside and see the sky, we have to realize that the heavens are speaking to us. Listen well! Hashem created us so that we should serve Him and merit great rewards, and each part of the world provides opportunities for growth.

- *Day following day their speech is expressed...* The purpose of every day is to learn more about Hashem, to think about His wonderful creations, and to say, "Thank You, Hashem, for everything."

- *They have no speech and they have no words... The*

times wondered how that tree came into existence? Have you contemplated that as great as the many accomplishments of science, scientists cannot duplicate even a "simple" tree? Each and every creation in this world is a collection of miracles from Hashem, created for our benefit.

- *Throughout the earth they extend...* He has set a tent in their midst for the sun. Everything in the universe works together so that the whole world is maintained in perfect harmony.

  The verse states that Hashem has provided the sun with a home, a place to which it returns daily, a "tent." Rashi learns that this refers to the atmospheric gases that encase the sun and protect us from its incredible heat. Thus, Hashem directs the sun's power to serve the world in exactly the right measure.

- *[The sun] is like a groom exiting his chuppah; it rejoices like a mighty warrior ready to run to battle.*

  In these two metaphors, the sun is portrayed as being proud and excited over its unique position as the provider of energy for the world, a great privilege and an awesome responsibility.

  In addition, the groom and the warrior can refer to the two fundamental approaches to serving Hashem that we learn from the Torah: love and fear of Hashem. A groom is happy to have found his mate, but he also needs to brace himself for the challenges of life that will confront him. The warrior, for his part, rejoices in the fact that he can show his loyalty to his nation and his king.

  Just as the groom is filled with great love for his new partner in life, we too must relate to Hashem with love. The soldier, on the other hand, approaches his mission with discipline, fear, and prayers — a true example of *yiras Hashem.*

- *...Nothing is hidden from its heat.* Every living being needs the sun to survive.

Now the chapter begins to discuss the spiritual

...

...tain is Hashem's wisdom, which is the most incredible, perfect, and infinite wisdom.

The Malbim explains that this is why we have a contrast here between the heavens, which declare and proclaim Hashem's glory, and the Torah, which is the source of all Creation — Hashem's blueprint for the universe.

- *The testimonies of Hashem are loyal, bringing wisdom to mankind.* This refers to all of the mitzvos, but most especially the mitzvah of Shabbos, which serves to testify that Hashem created the world in six days and rested on the seventh.

The luminaries make us wise by providing us with practical, hands-on training on learning and thinking over the truths of life and what Hashem expects of us. Just as the luminaries follow their "instructions" by staying in their orbits, we are to follow Hashem's Torah and thereby fulfill our role in Creation as well.

- *The orders of Hashem are upright…* We do not know all the meanings or reasonings behind every mitzvah. *Pekudei Hashem,* the orders of Hashem, refers to those mitzvos that we readily understand. They bring us greater joy because they are clear, logical, and bring immediate beneficial results.

  However, every mitzvah of Hashem, whether we are able to understand the reasoning behind it or not, is pure and illuminates our eyes. Without mitzvos, we would be living in darkness, not knowing what to do. The mitzvos guide us and direct us in fulfilling our purpose in life. That is why we say, "A mitzvah is [like] a candle [providing some light], and the Torah is [like] sunlight [which illuminates the entire world]" (*Mishlei* 6:23).

- *Fear of Hashem is pure…* We need to be afraid to sin, for the consequences are tragic. Fear of Hashem purifies us and brings us closer to Hashem.

- *More desirable than gold…* The Torah and mitzvos are more desirable than the best gold and the sweetest honey.

- *Your servant is careful and receives great rewards.* The word used for "reward" is "*eikev*" (עקב),

which has the *gematria* (numerical equivalent)

hidden errors. Even if a person has successfully avoided sin, he must be aware that this is an ongoing, continual battle for which he needs assistance from Hashem.

• *Also from intentional sins, please restrain Your servant…* We need to pray to Hashem for all of our needs, especially for the strength and wisdom to avoid sin.

• *May the sayings of my mouth and the expressions of my heart find favor before You, Hashem, my Rock and My Redeemer.* This verse is recited at the conclusion of every *Shemoneh Esrei.*

What are "the expressions of my heart"? These are thoughts that were not yet verbalized, yet are heard by Hashem anyway.

This chapter of *Tehillim,* chapter 19, is preceded by eighteen chapters of *Tehillim,* while its concluding verse, *"Yehiyu l'ratzon,"* is preceded by the eighteen *berachos* of *Shemoneh Esrei* (see *Berachos* 9b). Thus, we say these words at the conclusion of the *Shemoneh Esrei* to summarize our thoughts and ask Hashem to please listen to and accept all of our prayers.

ONE MOMENT SPOTLIGHT: There is so much for us to learn and to fulfill during our limited time on this earth. As we strive to do everything that we must do, we must also pray for Hashem's help in staying pure and in striving for perfection.

Consider this: When Hashem provides you with a great day, He expects to hear from you about it!

You can do it right now: "Thank You, Hashem, for all of Your ongoing help."

It is our duty to praise the Master of All, to appreciate the greatness of the Creator of the universe...
(Opening words of *Aleinu*)

The *Aleinu* prayer is recited three times a day, at the conclusion of *shacharis*, *minchah*, and *ma'ariv*, as well as at the end of *Kiddush Levanah*, *Birkas Ha-Chamah*, and a *bris milah* ceremony.

Aleinu consists of two paragraphs, each beginning with an *ayin* (in *Nusach Sefard*, the second paragraph actually begins with a *vav*, i.e., *vav* and then *ayin*) and ending with a *daled*. The letters *ayin-daled* spell עד, witness. The fact that there are two paragraphs beginning with *ayin* and ending with *daled* is a hint that are two "witnesses" involved, just as matters in Jewish law are established by the testimony of two witnesses. When we say *Aleinu*, we are serving as witnesses to the fact that Hashem is the Creator of the universe and everything in it.

This prayer summarizes our purpose in life and the goals we need to take with us until the next prayer service:

- *It is our duty to praise...* Praising Hashem is the purpose of life, for He is the Creator, Controller, and Master of All.

- *For He has not made us like the [other] nations...* The Jewish people are not like any of the other nations. We have unique potential, privileges, and responsibilities.

- *We bend our knees, bow, and acknowledge...* We bow down and express our thanks only to Hashem, the King of all kings.

- *True is our King, there is none besides Him...* He is the absolute truth, the Creator of all. There is no other like Hashem.

- *You shall know today and place it on your heart...* We need to keep internalizing this secret of the reality of the universe — Hashem runs it all, and He is in complete control.

Since *Aleinu* testifies that Hashem created the world, we should always try to say this prayer with concentration and joy.

The *Kolbo* (*siman* 16) writes that the words of this

prayer were composed by Yehoshua when the Jews

The second paragraph of *Aleinu* begins, "There-fore we hope to You, Hashem, to speedily see Your mighty splendor." This is a special mitzvah of hop-ing for Hashem's salvation, which is incumbent upon every Jew. It is written in first person, directed to Hashem, which shows our yearning to come to a new level of closeness to Hashem.

ONE MOMENT SPOTLIGHT: We often tend to rush from this to that without stop. Give your-self some time to think of the first two words of *Aleinu*, "*Aleinu leshabei'ach*, It is our duty to praise..." We are in this world to relate Hash-em's praises (see *Yeshayah* 43:21).

Consider spending one moment a day on this thought. After a few weeks you will discover that you have a whole new focus on life.

Chapter 9

KADDISH

The Kaddish prayer is repeated in various places in our prayers to highlight and reinforce our belief in Hashem's glory and might. It is worthwhile to learn the meaning of these words which we respond to every day in order to be able to say them with more *kavanah,* concentration. Although we will not be doing a line-by-line analysis of Kaddish here, we recommend that our readers do so on their own, to enhance their appreciation of this all-important prayer.

We will note, however, that in the first line of Kaddish we say, "May His great Name be magnified and sanctified." Our goal is to recognize that Hashem is behind everything.

At the conclusion of the first paragraph, everyone answers *"amen,"* which means we all agree that Hashem is the One and Only Creator and Controller.

Following *"amen,"* we say, "May His great Name be

tifying Hashem's Name. The commentators explain that this prayer serves to highlight and elevate the basic fundamental lessons we learn from the prayers we are concluding and to those we will be beginning. One of the reasons it is added to the *Birkas HaChamah* service is so that no one will think that we are practicing some sort of sun worship, *chas veshalom*. Our service is clearly a service to Hashem.

✦ ✦ ✦

In addition to being recited by the chazzan at various points in the prayer, Kaddish is also said by a mourner in his first year of mourning and on a *yahrtzeit*. Why should this prayer be the one designated for a mourner if it does not seem to refer to a deceased? Through reciting this prayer, the deceased person's children praise Hashem in the deceased person's place, thus bringing more glory of Hashem into the world. When the rest of the congregation joins in, this is a merit for the deceased and an elevation for his *neshamah*.

ONE MOMENT SPOTLIGHT: The Gemara offers a glimpse into the awesome power of Kaddish:

Anyone who responds [to Kaddish] with 'Amen (it is true and I fully agree), may His great Name be blessed forever and ever,' with all of his strength and concentration will merit to have any evil decrees against him torn up!

(*Shabbos* 119b)

Why is this so? Because such a person is demonstrating that he is completely focused on fulfilling his purpose in life.

PART II
THE MARVEL

The days of our years [on this earth] are seventy, and
if with strength, eighty; and their pride includes toil
and pain, for [they are] cut off swiftly and fly away.
(*Tehillim* 90:10)

This verse is recited every Shabbos morning as part of *Pesukei DeZimrah*. What are we saying here? Let us stop and consider these timeless words.

In the scope of eternity, our time on this earth is short. The years fly away swiftly. When a person is sixty or seventy years old, he may remember events from when he was a child. Even if they occurred half a century before, those fifty years seem like nothing, as if they happened just yesterday.

The sun rises and sets every day, but do we notice

it at all? We need to wake up and take notice before our time on this earth is up.

✦ ✦ ✦

The sun is an example of the Creator's unique kindness. In *Tehillim* (136:7), David HaMelech proclaims: "To the Maker of the great luminaries, His kindliness is everlasting." Similarly, we say, "The Heavens relate the glory of Hashem" (ibid. 19:2). Likewise, we find, "Hashem is a sun and a shield [for us]" (ibid. 84:12).

Imagine if someone were to invent a light bulb that provides light, heat, and also fills up the refrigerator with food. Such an inventor would become a billionaire in a short time. Hashem created such a light. Solar energy supplies life-giving light and heat, as well as photosynthesis which causes food to grow. All this was intended by Hashem to bring us to the recognition of His infinite kindliness so that we will praise and thank Him for everything.

The Talmud (*Chullin* 59b) tells of a Roman leader who demanded that a certain sage show him the Creator. The sage instructed the Roman to look into the sun. When the Roman said that it was impossible for him to do so, the sage responded, "Then how can you expect to see Hashem?" That is, if he could not even look directly at one of Hashem's creations, how

✦ ✦ ✦

Before and after the *Birkas HaChamah* service, it would be wise to think, and say, "Thank You, Hashem, for providing us with Your glorious sun for the last twenty-eight years."

✦ ✦ ✦

ONE MOMENT SPOTLIGHT: Take a minute now to consider the approximate dollar value of some of the benefits Hashem provides us with through the sun. Imagine the value of sunlight, warmth, and nutrients that are bestowed upon the entire world every single moment of the day. How much is that worth?

Ten billion dollars? Fifty billion? One hundred billion?

Too difficult? Think of one aspect of what

you receive from the sun and place a value on it — can you do it?

This should serve to enhance our appreciation of the sun, every single minute of the day.

How sweet is the light, how good it is for the eyes to see the sun!

(*Koheles* 11:7)

Every day, the sun provides us with light to see by and enjoy; life-saving warmth; life-giving vitamin D; photosynthesis, which sustains all vegetation; the days and the seasons; and countless other luxuries and necessities. Rav Avigdor Miller points out (*Awake My Glory*, para. 930) that 126 trillion horsepower of solar energy beams come down to the earth every second, causing millions of tons of water to rise as vapor, setting into motion air currents, that, together with the winds resulting from the earth's rotation, convey the rainclouds which provide water all over the world.

How can we thank Hashem for all of this? By focusing properly on the *Yotzer Ohr* blessing before we recite Shema every day, we can remember Hashem's goodness to us.

Let us study the *Yotzer Ohr* blessing, phrase by phrase, to glean some of the many gems contained in it:

- *Who forms light and creates darkness...* The sun is amazingly powerful. It showers us with millions of tons of solar energy that pour down every minute. But if it kept on nonstop, *chas veshalom*, we might get burnt. How would we deal with all that energy?

  Hashem has provided us with the perfect "on/off switch," called night! Plus, He created an automatic dimmer: the sun sets slowly as evening approaches so that we can adjust gradually to the change.

- *He makes peace...* Hashem makes the light and darkness complement each other — they cooperate, harmonizing with perfect compatibility.

- *And creates everything.* Why do we jump from light, darkness, and peace to "everything"?

  The sun is like an enormous battery that energizes all of life on earth.

  We can explain this based on a novel insight of Rav Avigdor Miller (*Praise My Soul*, para. 751):

  The creation of the heavens and earth was the greatest and most unique wonder in history, the unequaled marvel of Creation from

This teaches us that all of Creation is value-less without the creation of light with which to see!

The sole purpose of all of Creation is that we should see it and recognize the Creator.

Hashem made everything so that [we] should fear [i.e., be aware of] Him.

(*Koheles* 3:14)

- *He gives light to the earth and to the people who live upon it with mercy.* Hashem's light provides for the basic needs of the earth itself, and at the same time provides for its inhabitants, each with its own needs and requirements. It provides multiple benefits to countless recipients of all kinds, as we say in *Ashrei*, "Hashem is good to all" (*Tehillim* 145:9).

- *And in His goodness He renews constantly, daily,*

the work of Creation (ma'aseh vereishis). This is the same expression used in the blessing of *Birkas HaChamah*, recited once every twenty-eight years.

Thus, we see two aspects of Hashem's handiwork: (1) the daily appreciation of Hashem's world, as we say in the *Yotzer Ohr* blessing, and (2) the once-in-twenty-eight-year mention of *Birkas HaChamah*, when the sun's position returns to the way it was at the beginning of Creation.

This is an awesome idea. The fact that the *Anshei Knesses HaGedolah*, the Sages who composed our prayers, used the same expression for a once-in-twenty-eight-year event, as for our daily prayers, serves to teach us to wake up every day and recognize that Hashem creates a new world for us every day.

When we say the words *"ma'aseh vereishis"* in the *Yotzer Ohr* blessing every morning (this phrase actually appears twice in the blessing), we must remember: Hashem keeps on renewing the world for our benefit. Wow!!

- *How many are Your actions, Hashem — You make them all with wisdom; the world is filled with Your possessions.*

When we walk outside in the springtime and

ONE MOMENT SPOTLIGHT: Why does the Torah instruct us to light the Menorah in the Beis Ha-Mikdash every day? Surely Hashem does not need our insignificant amount of light to illuminate His Holy Temple.

Our Sages explain that the light in the Beis HaMikdash serves to teach us that Hashem considers even the small amount of light that we provide to be like the sun that illuminates the whole world.

If we fail to appreciate the greatness of the sun, we will end up dismissing our own greatness as well.

Chapter 12

GRATITUDE TO OUR CREATOR

Let us continue with our analysis of the blessing of *Yotzer Ohr*:

- *The King, Who is elevated above all...* Hashem is the only Creator and Controller of the entire universe. Everything else is His creation.

  One of the basic, fundamental teachings of the Torah is that we are obligated to "repay" our Benefactor for every benefit we receive by recognizing and thanking Him. Thus, every morning we must remember to be grateful for the sun and express our gratitude for it to the Creator.

  This extends to many other areas of life as well. If you happen to pass near the ocean, for example, you should think of the great miracle of the splitting of the sea and thank Hashem for splitting the Yam Suf and saving our nation

on us... At this point in the *berachah*, we take a break from praising Hashem for His creations and say instead, "With Your great mercy, have mercy on us." Why does this urgent plea for mercy appear in the middle of this *berachah*?

Rav Avigdor Miller, *zt"l*, explains (*Sing, You Righteous*, p. 285) that we are pleading with Hashem specifically to open our eyes to see His creations, so that we don't waste our lives living in spiritual darkness. Rav Miller compares walking outside on a sunny day to wading through piles of golden coins.

(Note: Although we would like to study every word of this *tefillah* in depth, time and space do not allow for it in this book. *B'ezras Hashem*, we hope to devote a future volume to this topic.)

✦ ✦ ✦

ONE MOMENT SPOTLIGHT: In Hebrew, the phrase for giving thanks is *hakaras hatov*, recognizing the good.

This concept is not limited to thanking Hashem for allowing us to view and experience His amazing world.

The Mishnah (*Avos* 1:6) teaches that friends are so valuable that we should "buy" them. If you have a good friend who lights up your day, take the time to thank Hashem for him or her — and thank your friend, too — and, further, ask Hashem to bless your friend with long life, happiness, and enjoyment from his children.

Hakaras hatov is very important. While a person may be humble and tell you that it's not necessary to pay or thank him for a favor he has done for you, it is, nevertheless, a fundmental Torah obligation to express your thanks. In this way, we train ourselves to remember also who the ultimate Giver is and to thank Him as well.

Every day is a new day, a time to start again. Every Rosh Chodesh is a new opportunity to start a new month. Every Rosh HaShanah is a time to resolve to be better for the coming year. However, it is important to remember that not everything happens at once. "One who grabs a little at a time will be successful" (*Sukkah* 5b).

One of the lessons to be learned from Hashem's creating a new world for us daily is to teach us how to approach life.

Even while doing something of great significance, such as learning or davening, we may sometimes become bored or tired. Often, however, our boredom and weariness stems from a mental or emotional attitude, rather than from physical exertion.

In contrast, when we are doing something new, we usually feel interested in it and enjoy ourselves more.

We get excited. People who enjoy their work don't get so tired from the actual work. It is worry, frustration, or disturbances that may tire them. This is one of the reasons that the Mishnah in *Avos* (1:10) teaches us "to love work." "Love your work" means to get absorbed in what you do, with the proper focus and attention. Give it your full and complete attention.

The challenge we have is to realize that every single morning Hashem bestows upon us a new day. If we internalize this reality, we can develop more energy, zest, and ongoing joy that can keep us going throughout the entire day.

Every day is a new opportunity to grow and develop in many ways.

But what do we do if we just don't feel like enjoying today as if it was a new day? In such a case, we are enjoined to act as if we feel that it is a new day. That is how we can train ourselves to eventually reach that level.

We can develop our initiative and enthusiasm to enjoy every new day that Hashem sends our way.

When we say the words, "He renews, with His goodness, every day, the work of Creation," we should be thankful and grateful for the new day, a new gift from Hashem.

ONE MOMENT SPOTLIGHT: One of the great hon

Chapter 14

AN OPPORTUNE TIME FOR PRAYER

May it be Hashem's will that we merit the light of the seven days of Creation.

(*Kiddush Levanah* prayer)

Every time we do a mitzvah of this nature, we should utilize the opportunity to talk to Hashem and ask Him for the things that our hearts desire.

"A mitzvah is [like] a candle, and Torah is [like] sunlight" (*Mishlei* 6:23). Rashi (on *Shabbos* 23b) teaches that this verse can refer to the mitzvos of lighting the Shabbos and Chanukah candles. Through the merit of lighting these candles, and fulfilling the accompanying laws and concepts, a couple will merit sons who will become Torah scholars, thus bringing light into the world. This is why the "*Yehi Ratzon*" prayer recited on Friday night after lighting the Shabbos candles includes a request to merit children who will become

moving into a new place, it is a good idea to focus on the following verse from *Tehillim* (127:1): "If Hashem will not build the house, in vain do the builders toil..."

During *Birkas HaChamah*, when we bless Hashem for the sun, we can also ask Him to provide us with a home that is saturated with Torah and mitzvos and to thank Him for helping us to come as far as we have.

> *Everything has its season, and there is a time for everything... A time to be born, and a time to die; a time to plant, and a time to uproot what is planted; a time to heal, and, a time to build; a time to cry and a time to laugh; a time to mourn and a time to dance; a time to scatter stones and a time to gather them in...a time to be silent and a time to speak...a time for war and a time for peace.*

> (*Koheles* 3:1)

No matter what stage of life we are at, there is always something to pray for. Let us utilize the opportunity of *Birkas HaChamah* to ask Hashem for help in all of these areas.

Every special occasion or milestone should be viewed as an opportunity to reflect on our lives and look back with gratitude to Hashem, and to look forward with renewed hope for the future. We all need such occasions from time to time to remind us to look at our lives with a fresh lens and to focus again on whatever area needs strengthening.

It is important to note that it is always appropriate to pray to Hashem. If you need special assistance, pray to Hashem now; do not wait for *Birkas Ha-Chamah*. Although we are focusing our attention on this ceremony as a point to look forward to, we are not suggesting that you delay your prayers for assistance until some time in the future. Act now! Prayer is always considered "timely."

✦ ✦ ✦

ONE MOMENT SPOTLIGHT: As we pray for our needs, we should also keep in mind the words of *Mesillas Yesharim*: the external inspires the internal. Hashem loves us and desires to help us. Act as if Hashem will help you and He will.

Look for the positive results and Hashem will

Our attitude is a very important aspect of life. Even if the light is shining, if we don't have the right attitude, we can lose the opportunity to benefit from the light. Thus, we should keep in mind, "A good heart is always at a banquet" (*Mishlei* 15:15), i.e., one with a good heart is always happy.

As we get up in the morning and get our wits about us, we should run to pray, in order to ask Hashem to please help us see the light and have a successful day!

Chapter 15
A FRESH START

Hashem gives us many chances to start over, to improve and do better.

Every morning we get a fresh start, a chance to begin again.

But the day of *Birkas HaChamah*, with its once-in-twenty-eight-years opportunity, is a special day, one that does not repeat itself for a long time.

A person should always say, "The world was created for me."

(*Sanhedrin* 37a)

When we contemplate the sun and its creation, we can use the opportunity to both review the past twenty-eight years of our lives and analyze whether we have always acted as we wanted to and consider the future and what we hope to accomplish, *b'ezras Hashem*, in the next twenty-eight years.

✦   ✦   ✦

This process should not be taken lightly. If we begin preparing now for the upcoming *Birkas Ha-Chamah*, we will be able to zero in on what we must do to correct and avoid past mistakes, as well as to turn them into learning opportunities.

Things are happening around us all the time. However, it is necessary to not only see what is happening but to also stop for a moment and analyze what has happened. Hashem keeps sending opportunities knocking on our door. We must not ignore them.

✦   ✦   ✦

ONE MOMENT SPOTLIGHT: One of the greatest lessons of this once-in-twenty-eight-years encounter is learning to stop and notice that which may seem obvious.

The sun looks pretty much the same every

day. Even on this special day which occurs only once in twenty-eight years the sun does not look any different to us — yet our Sages say, "Stop and say a *berachah*."

We need to learn to listen, pay attention, and think more.

Every day may seem the same as the one that came before it, but every day is not the same. It's up to us to strive to make it better, different, more enlightening...by learning a new Torah thought and reviewing old ones, by giving someone a call who might need a boost, by saying hello to someone you pass in the street, by doing a mitzvah, by giving *tzedakah*, by saying a special *tefillah* to Hashem. We can always utilize our lives to serve Hashem.

Even if you don't have the time to stop and smell the flowers, stop and look at them, even for a second, and remind yourself that Hashem created them for you!

The opportunity to recite *Birkas HaChamah* is special; it will not repeat itself for another twenty-eight years.

What can you do or say to take advantage of this rare opportunity?

First of all, you can remember to take advantage of the blessing itself. You can reject the attitude, "I'll recite the *Birkas HaChamah* service quickly and get it over with," and say instead, "Let me prepare as fully as I can beforehand in order to make the most of this unique opportunity."

If not now, when?

(*Avos* 1:14)

This may be an appropriate time for you to set goals for the future:

- If you are not married, set the goal to get married, *b'ezras Hashem*, way before the next *Birkas HaChamah*, on April 8, 2037. (If you are an older single, you may consider asking a *shailah* and setting yourself a sixty-to-ninety day deadline for getting married. A *rav* once said, "If someone put half a million dollars in the bank for you to access on the day you got married, with a four-week deadline, would you make it?" Hashem's rewards are greater!)

- Consider setting up a Torah learning program for yourself. Even if you were to start with a minimum program of memorizing one *mishnah* a year until the next *Birkas HaChamah*, you would have learned and memorized twenty-eight *mishnayos*!

- Decide to focus on studying and mastering the meaning of one segment of the daily prayers (for example, *Aleinu*).

- Find a teacher or a mentor, if you do not already have one.

- Decide to change, control, and master at least one negative *middah* (character trait).

- Resolve to be kinder to people that you currently have difficulty in getting along with.

- Be a good friend to even one person, as a start.

Establish some goals and set concrete steps to ac

apply from these pages to improve your life over the next several years.

For example, there was once a full-page advertisement in a newspaper addressed to people who, *baruch Hashem*, are able to leave shul during the recitation of *Yizkor*.

When people leave shul during *Yizkor*, they have a brief recess from davening. How can they use this time wisely and avoid disturbing those who remain in shul and are praying to Hashem for merits for their departed relatives? There are many possibilities. For example, you can:

- Thank HaKadosh Baruch Hu for the good fortune that you have to still remain outside during *Yizkor*!

- Say a chapter or two of *Tehillim*.

- Learn a *mishnah*.

- Learn some of the *halachos* of honoring parents

or the laws of *lashon hara*, both of which guarantee a long life.

• Try to think of a *shidduch* for someone in need.

The opportunities are endless; you just need to think of them and grab them!

ONE MOMENT SPOTLIGHT: Our text in the Talmud (*Berachos* 59b) uses the words, "*Oseh vereishis* — Who makes Creation," for *Birkas HaChamah*, but the commentators say that this should read, "*Oseh ma'aseh vereishis* — Who makes *the work of* Creation."

The word *ma'aseh*, work or action, is significant, for it hints at one of the purposes of Creation: to take action. The more we act with *zerizus*, energetic action, the more Hashem will help us.

The Mishnah (*Avos* 1:17) compares action and thought in the following statement: "The *midrash* (analysis) is not primary; the most important thing is action."

You may discover a *d'var Torah* that can change your life, but if you do not take action to implement and apply the message, it can be lost.

One of the blessings we say every morning is "*Pokei'ach Ivrim* — [Blessed are You, Hashem] Who gives sight to the blind."

The question is asked, does a blind person recite this *berachah*? The answer is yes. Why? One reason is that he benefits from the assistance of others who are able to see and thus are able to assist and guide him, too. (See *Mishnah Berurah* 46:25.)

"One may not place a stumbling block before a blind person" (*Vayikra* 19:14). This refers also to the prohibition against giving bad advice to another person.

Each person has the ability to help others, to illuminate their lives with physical assistance, emotional assistance, and added knowledge, in the form of insights into various subjects and in various ways.

If your friend needs assistance and you can provide that assistance, try to make every effort to help out.

Our Sages call this concept, "A candle for one, a candle for one hundred" (*Shabbos* 122a). Just as the sun shines for one person, so does it shine for millions. This serves as a model for us, since if we help a person in need, this in turn will lead to helping many others.

This idea is also related to the concept in *Avos* (4:2): "One mitzvah pulls another [in its wake]." When a person is in "mitzvah motion," it is easier to remain in motion and to keep on helping more people. We need to always keep the lights of inspiration burning.

We can also learn from this about the importance of the mitzvah of *tochechah*, rebuke. When you see that someone is not acting correctly and you feel that he or she may be receptive to your thoughts, you have an obligation to approach him or her, in private, and address your concerns for their benefit.

Giving *tochechah*, however, requires the utmost tact. If you are successful, the person may be thankful. If not, he or she may become resentful towards you (although obviously this is a mistake on their part). We must be careful to avoid such a situation, and not give *tochechah* to those who will be antagonistic, as we learn from Shlomo HaMelech, "Do not rebuke a scoffer lest he hate you; rebuke a wise person and he will love you" (*Mishlei* 9:8).

...gael Miller would say, "When you come home and it's hot in the kitchen, you can be sure that your wife is preparing a delicious meal."

Hashem utilizes the weather for many purposes, including to prepare delicious foods for people all over the world.

If people complain about the weather, it is considered as propaganda against Hashem! We need to say, "This too is for our benefit. Thank You, Hashem!"

Chapter 18

GREETINGS

Every morning, *baruch Hashem*, the sun greets us. Even if there is no one else around, our spirits are uplifted when we see that the sun is shining. It makes us feel better.

We can all bring sunshine to others if we make this concept a part of our character.

Receive every person with a cheerful facial expression.
(*Avos* 1:15)

Be first to greet every person.
(Ibid. 4:15)

Many times we leave the house in the morning hoping for a sunny day. Yet people often go out looking for a sunny day and forget to take their smile with them.

Without your smile, you may have just ruined

your own day and that of others. Your lack of a smile

If two stores sell the same type of merchandise at similar costs, which store do you choose to patronize?

You will most likely choose the store that has the friendlier atmosphere, where the clerks smile at you and make you feel welcome. Even if the prices in this store are higher, most people will prefer shopping there because the clerks seem to care about them and are nicer to them. The extra costs are outweighed by the friendliness of the establishment.

Similarly, the sun makes us happy and helps us smile more. Smiling gives us more energy and better health.

ONE MOMENT SPOTLIGHT: There are numerous benefits to a smile:

- A smile costs nothing, but it is worth a lot.

- It takes a moment, but its effects can last a lifetime.

- It creates happiness, goodwill, friendship, and cheer.

- It is a balm to all, an antidote to trouble.

- It is a small curve that can straighten things out.

How many times do we walk into shul in the morning and see people who seem unhappy? If we lighten up and smile more, in emulation of Hashem's ways, we will not only cheer up others but also gain significant benefits for ourselves.

Try it and see!

Does the sun move?

Although it appears to us that it does not move, with the *Birkas HaChamah* blessing we acknowledge, among many other things, that it does move, in a sense, for we say the blessing because the sun has returned to the same position it first occupied at the time of Creation.

Appearances are difficult to alter in our intellect or memory. We often find it difficult to reconcile what we believe happened with what actually happened, even though it is a mitzvah to judge every person favorably. An optical illusion can serve as a model for this all-important mitzvah, by reminding us that just because something seems to be one way that doesn't mean that it necessarily is.

It is not difficult to cause the wrong impression. Unfortunately, it may take years to correct a misimpression that we have made or caused. Twenty-eight years? We hope not. But if it does happen, we can still move on.

Rabbi Akiva teaches that the greatest rule of the Torah is to "love our fellowman as ourselves" (Rashi, *Sifra* on *Vayikra* 19:18).

If we have done something wrong, we generally don't hold ourselves guilty for twenty-eight years, or more. We try to rationalize our behavior and look for every possible excuse. Applying the mitzvah of *v'ahavta l'rei'acha kamocha*, we should do the same for our spouses, family members, friends, and coworkers.

✦ ✦ ✦

Is clean sea water pure or polluted?

For fish it is perfect, but for humans it is undrinkable and harmful.

How something appears and how something really is can be quite different — but it also depends for who and for what.

The sun provides us with a shadow throughout the day. Is the shadow a reflection of who we are? Obviously, the answer is no. But it looks like us. It is an imitation of us, albeit a superficial one, a mere look-alike.

Our shadows serve to remind us: Develop your

internal essence. Don't just be a shadow of yourself!

grow and master change, and more.

- The river also changes: the water keeps on flowing, and the nature of the river changes with it. Sometimes the water is high, sometimes it is low; sometimes the current is swift, while other times it is slow.

Let us remember this every time we are confronted with a challenge or an obstacle: The reason why Hashem presents us with these challenges is to keep us moving, to keep us changing. If we take the challenge and use the opportunity to grow, we can become a new person — and a more positive one — every single day.

Chapter 20
A SPHERE OF INFLUENCE

The sun is 93 million miles from the earth, yet we are affected by its warmth and light, in just the right measure, every single day.

In the same way, we all have an influence on those around us, whether we realize it or not. Our sphere of influence may seem smaller than the sun's, but we still impact on our family members, friends, neighbors, shul-mates, and coworkers every single day. The ripple effect of a single action can be incredible.

What can we do with this knowledge? It is worthwhile for us to evaluate all of our actions, both *bein adam laMakom* and *bein adam lechaveiro*, on a regular basis, so that we may be sure we are having a good influence on others, and not, *chas veshalom*, the opposite.

The biggest influence that we have is on our children. The way we treat them, and the character traits

nomenon of children, *Rachmana litzlan*, going off the *derech*, it is imperative to model good behavior both inside the home and out. If we fail to do this, we will have ourselves to take to task if our children, *chas veshalom*, choose a different path for themselves.

While in general one should not publicize his own mitzvos, it is important to do so at times for educational purposes, especially with regard to our own children.

✦ ✦ ✦

Hashem causes the world to operate under a system called *middah keneged middah*, measure for measure. If we help someone in a certain way, Hashem will cause others to help us in similar ways. Thus, if we, for example, go out of our way to treat elderly parents with the proper honor and respect, we will find that one day, *b'ezras Hashem*, our children will treat us with honor and respect.

You can turn on your power of encouragement and change someone's life by giving him something that will help bring him to the right place — for example, a book of Torah thoughts or a series of Torah lectures to listen to. The possibilities are endless — don't delay; start today!

> *On the path one desires to go, he will be led.*
> (*Makkos* 10b)

Even if our goals for self-improvement seem insurmountable, we must not give up — Hashem will help us keep going and achieve our goals if we turn on the "lights" of desire and determination.

✦   ✦   ✦

ONE MOMENT SPOTLIGHT: The sun is not only a physical benefit, providing endless essentials; it also provides us with many messages and insights and much inspiration. Consider:

> *The sun rises in the east*
> *and sets in the west.*
> *It stays close to the horizon in the winter,*
> *closer to the zenith in the summer.*
> *Who sets its course?*
> *Hashem.*

If it began to rise in the west or if it stopped

PART III

THE MESSAGE

As we mentioned above (chapter 2, "The Halachos of *Birkas HaChamah*"), if the sun is covered by clouds on the morning of *Birkas HaChamah*, one may only recite the blessing if the sun's impression can be seen. If one cannot see the impression of the sun at sunrise, he can wait up to noon to say the *berachah*.

> *Who is wise? He who foresees the future.*
>
> (*Tamid* 32a)

Things don't always occur the way we hope or expect them to. Thus, we would do well to anticipate several possible scenarios for any given situation and prepare accordingly.

This concept is not limited to events, but is also applicable to our interactions with others. Before you act or speak, try to visualize the effect your words or actions will have on the other person or people. If you think about your listeners' sensitivities in advance, you will be able to avoid unintentionally offending another person.

What if it does rain or is too cloudy on the morning of *Birkas HaChamah*? How are we to react? Although it is natural to be frustrated or irritated when our plans don't work out, we should look at it from a different perspective: Hashem may be testing us to see how we react to adversity in general!

When things seem to go wrong, are we patient, or do we grumble and complain? Do we start yelling and screaming at those who happen to be present? Do we blame others?

If we find ourselves overreacting to minor delays or mishaps, now may be a good time to learn how to improve in this area, bearing in mind the famous teaching of Rabbi Akiva, "Everything the All-Merciful does is for the good" (*Berachos* 60b).

ONE MOMENT SPOTLIGHT: When the sun is hiding, we get to see the clouds, the rain, or the

how worthwhile, may not leave time for other projects or pursuits.

When the sun is covered, we can take it as a sign that it is time to reevaluate:

- *Are we overshadowing the group?* Is your ego getting in the way of your growth or the growth of others?

- *Are we making too much noise?* Do you make so much noise at work or at home that it prevents others from concentrating and excelling?

- *Are we using too much of a dominant "spice"?* Do you approach everything with the same attitude, without considering that the same spice doesn't always bring out the right flavor for every dish?

- *Are we too preoccupied with a certain activity,*

to the exclusion of all others? Are you a workaholic who concentrates so much on his work that he forgets about the other mitzvos that Hashem is waiting for him to accomplish? Is your love for exercise (*"v'nishmartem me'od"*) preventing you from learning and davening with *kavanah*? There are many ways in which we need to improve; let's not forget one in our eagerness to do another.

What if you got up on time, went to minyan, and did everything you could, but, nevertheless, for whatever reason, you missed reciting *Birkas HaChamah*?

I mentioned this to an acquaintance of mine and he said, "Oh, well, better luck next time." Next time — that will be in another twenty-eight years. Who knows what will be between now and then?

In *Parashas Beha'aloscha*, the Torah describes how a group of people were unable to bring the *korban Pesach* on time. They approached Moshe Rabbeinu and asked if something could be done. Moshe inquired of Hashem and was told that people who were ritually unclean or too far away from the Mishkan or Mikdash on the fourteenth day of Nissan could bring the *korban Pesach* one month later, on the fourteenth day of Iyar. This day, called "Pesach Sheini," is a makeup day for those who missed this great mitzvah opportunity. We see from this that if we ask for another opportunity to do a mitzvah, we may get it.

A friend of mine was once in a shul for *minchah* on Pesach Sheini, and the rabbi of the shul related that once, many years before, his uncle (his father's brother) was about to marry off a child, but, unfortunately, the uncle's father (this rabbi's grandfather) had just passed away. The uncle very much wanted to go to his son's wedding. He asked a *shailah* whether he could attend and was told that he should not go, but that Hashem would bless him so that he would be able to attend many more *simchos*. This is exactly what happened: this uncle lived to attend the weddings of many of his grandchildren.

ONE MOMENT SPOTLIGHT: If someone tells you, "Opportunity only knocks once," you can teach them the story of Pesach Sheini. Hashem may give us a second opportunity if we ask for it.

This is a great lesson for all areas of life. Hashem provides us with opportunities, again and again, all over. We each have our unique potential to develop and actualize. If we "lose" one opportunity, we must keep our eyes, and hearts, open for the next one that comes.

Chapter 23
A UNIQUE OPPORTUNITY FOR BLESSING

Each Hebrew letter has a corresponding numerical value, called "*gematria.*" The Hebrew letters for the number twenty-eight are *kaf* and *ches* (*kaf* equals twenty and *ches* equals eight, for a total of twenty-eight), which together spell the word *koach*, strength.

Interestingly, the *Birkas HaChamah* service concludes with Kaddish, which includes the phrase, "*Yehei sh'mei rabbah mevorach le'olam u'le'olmei olmaya* — May His great Name be blessed forever and ever," which has a total of twenty-eight letters.

Our Sages teach that one of the reasons that this important phrase contains twenty-eight letters is in order to symbolize that we are praising Hashem's "*koach*" as the Source of All Power!

Similarly, the Baal HaTurim on *Bereishis 1:1* points

There are many blessings and salutations that we give throughout the Jewish year. For example, on Rosh HaShanah we say, *"Shanah tovah"* or "A good, *gebentched* year" (a year of blessings); on festivals, we say, *"Chag samei'ach"* or "Good *yom tov"*; on Rosh Chodesh, we say *"Chodesh tov"* or "A good *chodesh"*; and many say, *"Zie gezunt"* (you should be healthy) upon parting company. What should one say at the end of the *Birkas HaChamah* service?

Rabbi Avigdor Miller, *zt"l*, would often say that it is a great mitzvah to bless other Jews regularly, in many ways. We would therefore like to suggest that you consider blessing your fellow congregants and others with something related to the topic of strength.

Before you part company, *im yirtzeh Hashem*, on April 8, 2009, contemplate saying a strength-related *berachah* to your neighbor, keeping in mind that you will not have the same time-related opportunity for another twenty-eight years.

Think about what you know about the person you are blessing and ask Hashem to help him with his particular needs. For example:

- "Over the next twenty-eight years, may Hashem grant you all of your wishes for Torah, *parnassah* (livelihood), children, health, success..."

- "Over the next twenty-eight years, may Hashem grant you the strength and resources to marry off your children to suitable Torah scholars."

- "Over the next twenty-eight years, may Hashem grant you strength to learn and disseminate much Torah."

This is our blessing to you:

Over the next twenty-eight years, and beyond, may Hashem grant you the strength to do all that you need to do to raise a family and learn much Torah.

> *Those who hope to Hashem will have renewed strength.*

> (*Yeshayah* 40:31)

ONE MOMENT SPOTLIGHT: Hashem has various

one have the same test: to focus on serving Hashem with whatever means he was given.

A person whose life is only about his bank balance is in a sad situation.

Who is truly wealthy? One who rejoices with his portion.

(*Avos* 4:1)

The sun is a great part of our portion, and we must rejoice with it every day!

Chapter 24
LIGHTEN UP!

Another lesson we learn from the sun is to "lighten up" — to stop worrying so much and relax and enjoy the day. Lightening up can make all the difference in our lives.

At times, we get uptight about petty situations. It is important to remember not to take everything so seriously. By lightening up, we regain our perspective on life and retain our sense of humor. We cannot let the clouds block the sunshine and obscure our vision.

Worry and regret do have their place in Torah life with the mitzvah of *teshuvah*, but we have to learn to balance our perspective and not ruin our day by complaining and thereby compounding our problems.

Slow down and relax. Have *bitachon*, trust in Hashem, Who is running the world. He sends the sun out early every morning and we need to say, "Thank

You, Hashem, for another wonderful day!"

and that "all that the All-Merciful does is for the good" (*Berachos* 60b). We can keep our cool, remain positive, and think creatively.

"What does Hashem want me to do now?"

The *Mesillas Yesharim* (chapter 19) teaches us that joy is a component of the mitzvah to love Hashem, which is one of the six constant mitzvos. Thus, serving Hashem with joy is an ongoing mitzvah that can help us get to where Hashem wants us to go.

Chapter 25
BACKGROUND LIGHT

Hashem's creation of sunlight is very unique and loaded with profound, infinite wisdom.

Although sunlight is very bright, we don't necessarily direct our attention to it all day long — it is there, but it is in the background. In this sense, sunlight serves as a gentle, background light, which is both calming and energizing.

Thus, we can learn from the sun to be calm and relaxed, and yet at the same time joyful and enthusiastic about life.

There are many types of light.

Indoor lighting is a wonderful convenience. Nevertheless, sometimes we need sunlight to really see things clearly. For example, if a person is shopping for a suit or a dress that has to be a certain color, it is often difficult to see whether he's found the right

The *mishnah* in *Avos* teaches us one of the secrets to becoming wealthy: "Love your work" (*Avos* 1:10).

A person will succeed not just because he offers better services and lower prices, but because he loves what he does.

When you don't focus only on making money, but rather you have learned to love what you do and have placed the goal of making money in the background (like the sun), you will succeed more.

There is another secret to wealth.

> *Give a tenth [of your income] to charity so that you will become wealthy.*

(*Taanis* 9a)

When a person gives charity, he accomplishes two things: (1) he helps others, and (2) he helps himself.

A person who gives charity realizes that he can be like the sun and that his desires do not always have to be in the foreground, but must sometimes be in the background.

Acts of kindness fall in the same category — put your wants and desires in the background and think about helping someone else. "Do the will of Hashem as if it were your will, so that He will do your will as if it were His will" (*Avos* 2:4).

✦ ✦ ✦

ONE MOMENT SPOTLIGHT: It is important to be passionate about Torah and mitzvah goals. At the same time, we must not act in a manner that could be described as frantic.

A Jew should always act in a modest, gentle, appropriate way, a way that encourages others to emulate him. In this way, he can remain in the background, like the sun, yet the light of the Torah will shine forth from his actions.

In most places of the globe, the sun sets every night. Yet the time it sets is not always the same — depending on the time of year, it can be earlier in the evening or later in the evening, or even well into the night.

One of the powerful messages Hashem is sending us with each sunset is "Be willing to change." In the summer, the days are longer, and in the winter, the days are shorter. The sunlight itself is not always the same.

Each of us must consider what changes we need to make to our lives in order to create more positive situations.

Do you need to make changes in your interactions with your family members?

Do you need to make adjustments in the way you interact with your friends, relatives, employees, or coworkers?

Do you need to make changes in your Torah study?

Do you need to change your priorities in life and give more time to things you have previously neglected?

Every night is an opportunity to change something that needs changing.

People may tell you it's the same old sun. Yet the *Birkas HaChamah* blessing teaches us that even though it's an "old" sun, Hashem causes it to renew itself every day.

Throughout history, inventors have looked at old ways of doing things and analyzed whether they are the most time and cost efficient. They have tried new ways, time after time, and succeeded in changing the lives of many.

We can do the same. Don't let your habits blind you to new ways of doing things — there are always ways to improve on what we do and how we do it. Try it today!

✦   ✦   ✦

ONE MOMENT SPOTLIGHT: The setting of the sun also serves as a hint to us that we cannot work all night. In order to serve Hashem properly, a person has to watch his health and make sure not to push himself too hard.

we must constantly be aware of Hashem, who provides for all of our needs. Though we may seem to be missing out on some valuable working time, Hashem will, *im yirtzeh Hashem*, allow us to make it up later on in the day or the next day.

A break is not always a bad thing! On the contrary, it can remind us of our Creator, who is constantly helping us and on our side!

Chapter 27

AS SURE AS THE SUN RISES

Hashem made the sun rise today and, *im yirtzeh Hashem*, He will do so tomorrow, as well.

The concept of *bitachon*, faith in Hashem, is beautifully presented in *Tehillim* 23 by David HaMelech:

> *Hashem is my Shepherd; I lack nothing. He lays me down in lush meadows [referring to rest and food] and leads me alongside tranquil waters [referring to drink]… Even if I walk in the Valley of Death, I will not fear anything, for You [Hashem] are with me… You prepare my table before my enemies, You anointed my head with oil, [and] my cup is overflowing.*

From the sun's constant cycle, we learn not to worry because Hashem is in charge.

Every morning, as the sun rises again, Hashem

As the *Mesillas Yesharim* declares, "People were created to rejoice with Hashem..." (*Mesillas Yesharim*, ch. 1).

One of the great, outstanding messages of the sun is that Hashem has planted opportunities to see the light all around us.

Instead of seeing only problems, look for the possible solutions Hashem has waiting for you, and you will be able to see a whole new picture.

✦　✦　✦

ONE MOMENT SPOTLIGHT: Faith in Hashem is the first of the fundamental tenets of Judaism. The first of the Rambam's Thirteen Principles of Faith states: "I believe with complete faith that the Creator, blessed is His Name, creates and guides all of Creation, and that He alone made, makes, and will make everything."

When things appear to go wrong, we may

tend to blame another person or an external factor. However, the proper attitude is to realize that Hashem is constantly in control of this world. It is our duty to remember this and to contemplate what we may have done to bring this challenging or troublesome event upon us. If we recognize that our own actions may be at fault, we must try to rectify the situation.

Hashem keeps on opening doors for us — but not always the way we envisioned them! We need to "see" Hashem's actions and read His messages to us.

(Note: If something happens that is not the way we hoped or expected and we are not able to discern why, we should seek advice from a competent rabbi or a knowledgable friend.)

How many days, weeks, or months are left until the coming *Birkas HaChamah*? How much time can you allocate daily or weekly to this mitzvah, using the guidelines set forth in this book?

Proper preparation, a thorough look into all of the aspects of this mitzvah, and learning all of the sources available to us, will provide significant results.

Even if you invest only twenty hours into preparing for this once-in-twenty-eight-year mitzvah, you will gain a priceless investment that can remain with you for many years.

If you have children, consider teaching them about the significance of *Birkas HaChamah*, too. You can even go through the chapters of this book with them. At the same time, ask Hashem to give you the strength and good health to be able to guide them for many more years to come.

If you are a rebbe or a teacher, you can consider devoting a three-to-six week program to this subject.

This book can serve as a springboard for many class discussions that will greatly enhance your students' appreciation of the mitzvah.

Even if you do not become an expert on this subject, you can spread the word that this special occasion is coming and that people can use it to implement the ideas contained here.

If not now, when?

(*Avos* 1:14)

✦ ✦ ✦

ONE MINUTE SPOTLIGHT: What is your "sun"? What is the great dream that fills your life?

There are many Torah and mitzvah goals that can be the "suns" in our lives.

We have to look around and see what areas and concerns are priorities for us. Are we making the Torah and mitzvos our priorities, or *chas veshalom*, are there other things that take precedence over them?

The *Mesillas Yesharim* (ch. 1) teaches us the three purposes of life: (1) To fulfill mitzvos, (2) to serve Hashem, and (3) to withstand tests.

If we succeed in keeping these three goals uppermost in our mind, we will be able to sanctify Hashem's Name in every area of our lives.

Have you ever read about people digging for treasure? At times people find great amounts of hidden treasure in the most ordinary surroundings.

This is one of the lessons of the sun: It appears to be "ordinary," for we see it all the time, *baruch Hashem*. However, there are endless hidden treasures in it. As we recognize Hashem's light, we can proclaim our heartfelt thanks to the great Source of all Creation.

✦   ✦   ✦

The book *Selected Writings* by Rav Shimon Schwab, *zt"l* (C.I.S. Publishers, 1988) contains an essay entitled "Three Times *Birkas HaChamah*." In this essay, the Rav wrote of his experiences in 1925/5685, 1953/5713, and 1981/5741.

Rav Schwab concludes the essay with the message

that *Birkas HaChamah* is an expression of *emunah*, faith in Hashem — our conviction that the universe was not always here. It was created out of nothing, through Hashem's infinite wisdom and will.

The Jewish nation is also called "Reishis" — the first, or the beginning (see the first *Rashi* in *Bereishis*) and like the sun we are instructed to become a "light unto the nations." May we merit to fulfill our purpose, every day of the year.

We would like to conclude this book with the blessing the *kohanim* are instructed to recite in blessing the congregation:

> *May Hashem bless you and protect you. May He cause His light to shine upon you and be gracious to you. May He raise His countenance to you and grant you peace!*
>
> (*Bemidbar* 6:24–26)

We would like to extend a blessing that your planning go well and that you succeed in reciting *Birkas HaChamah* with new understanding this year and in future years, with Hashem's help.

1 MINUTE MESSAGES

Take a minute to discover the wisdom of the prophets.
Learn how their messages can transform your life.

Thousands of prophets shared their prophecies with the Jewish people. Only fifty-five had their words preserved for eternity. Their messages transcend the passing of time; their truth and practical wisdom is revealed in every generation. Now, in just a minute, you can discover the wisdom of the prophets and learn how their messages can transform your life. Discover their eternal messages in this pocket-sized treasure trove of wisdom.

To order, call 1-800-237-7149
or order online at www.targum.com